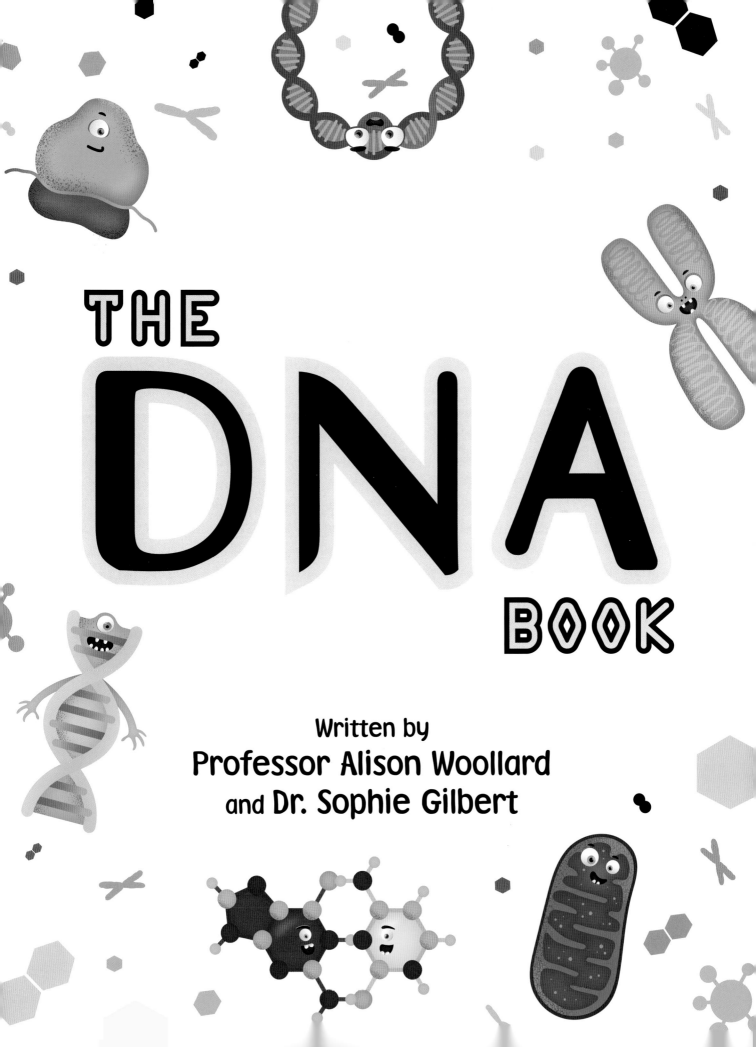

THE DNA BOOK

Written by
Professor Alison Woollard
and **Dr. Sophie Gilbert**

Contents

DK Penguin Random House

Written by Professor Alison Woollard and Dr. Sophie Gilbert
Consultant Dr. Vilaiwan Fernandes

Senior editor Jolyon Goddard
Project art editor Emma Hobson
Art editor Polly Appleton
US senior editor Shannon Beatty
US editor Margaret Parrish
Additional editorial Seeta Parmar, Olivia Stanford
Illustration Mark Clifton, Bettina Myklebust Stovne

Jacket coordinator Issy Walsh
Jacket designer Emma Hobson
Producer, pre-production David Almond
Senior producer Basia Ossowska
Managing editors Laura Gilbert, Jonathan Melmoth
Managing art editor Diane Peyton Jones
Picture researcher Sakshi Saluja
Creative directors Clare Baggaley, Helen Senior
Publishing director Sarah Larter

Educational consultant Jennifer Lane

First American Edition 2020
Published in the United States by DK Publishing
1745 Broadway, 20th Floor, New York, NY 10019

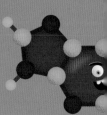

There are some **tricky words** that describe DNA in this book! Check the **glossary** if you come across any you're not sure about.

DK books are available at special discounts
when purchased in bulk for sales promotions,
premiums, fund-raising, or educational use.
For details, contact: DK Publishing Special Markets
1745 Broadway, 20th Floor, New York, NY 10019
SpecialSales@dk.com

Printed and bound in China

For the curious
www.dk.com

MIX
Paper | Supporting
responsible forestry
FSC™ C018179

This book was made with Forest
Stewardship Council™ certified
paper–one small step in DK's
commitment to a sustainable future.
For more information go to
www.dk.com/our-green-pledge

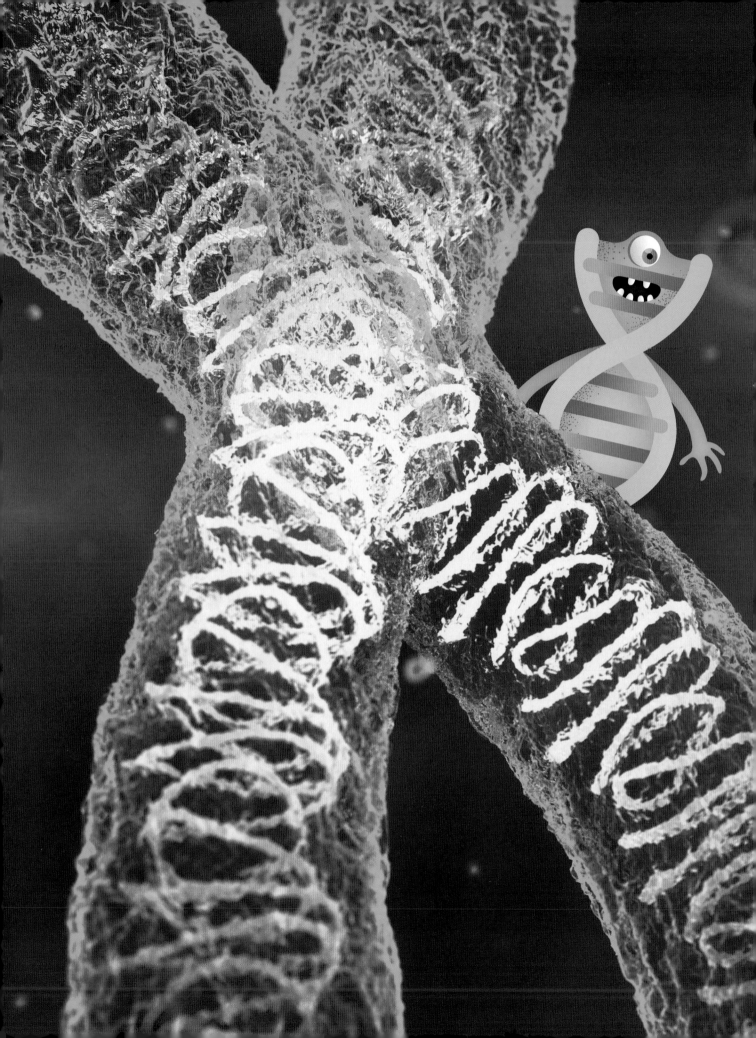

Introduction

Life is the greatest show on Earth, and we humans have the extraordinary privilege of having brains large enough to begin to understand it. Some life-forms are microscopic, while others are so big they can be seen from space. There are plants that eat animals, and bacteria that live in scalding-hot water. Some animals spend their lives entirely in the dark, while many others live underwater. **The secret of all this amazing diversity is DNA**.

DNA is the molecule that holds the **code for life**, from bats to beetles, and from mushrooms to mammoths. We all rely on it to **grow, survive, and reproduce**. Read on to find out what DNA is and what it can do—and what happens when it gets **mutated**!

Professor Alison Woollard   Dr. Sophie Gilbert

What is **DNA?**

DNA stands for **d**eoxyribo**n**ucleic **a**cid (dee-ox-ee-ry-boe-new-klay-ik a-sid). It's the chemical that makes up your genes, which **contain the instructions that make you who you are**, from the color of your eyes to the size of your feet.

Double helix
The twisted shape of DNA is called a double helix.

DNA

DNA is made up of three different things: sugar, phosphate, and bases. These are joined together to make one really long chain that forms a shape called a double helix. DNA has a strong structure and can store information for a long time.

Bases
Pairs of bases run along the inside of DNA.

DNA SEQUENCE

Genome
A complete set of your DNA is called your genome. The genomes of different organisms, or living things, can be very different sizes.

Genes

Certain sections of DNA make up your genes, which are responsible for all your characteristics. We have about 20,000 genes—and so do worms!

FRIEDRICH MIESCHER

DNA was discovered by a Swiss scientist named Friedrich Miescher. He was investigating white blood cells, which he collected from pus-covered bandages at a nearby hospital. From these he extracted a substance he called "nuclein." Nuclein later became nucleic acid, and today it is known as deoxyribonucleic acid (DNA).

Miescher discovered DNA in the late 1860s, but he didn't know what it did in the body.

DNA code lives forever!

Even when you're gone, your DNA code will live forever in your family.

Backbone
Sugar and phosphate units make up the outer backbone of DNA.

Bases are the code of life

The order, or sequence, of the bases makes up the information in the DNA. There are four different bases in DNA, called A, T, C, and G. They make up the code for all life on Earth.

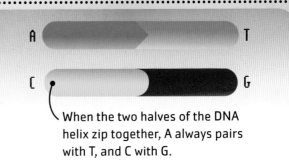

When the two halves of the DNA helix zip together, A always pairs with T, and C with G.

Where is DNA in my body?

Each **tiny cell** in your body contains a complete copy of your **genome**. Amazingly, if you stretched out your genome it would be **6 ft 6in (2 m) long**, so it has to be packed up very tightly to fit inside your cells.

Gene
A gene is a length of DNA that contains the code for a particular characteristic, such as hair color.

Tracking down your DNA

We need to delve deep inside your cells to find the DNA. It is kept inside a special compartment of the cell called the nucleus. Here, your DNA is wound up very tightly to keep it safe.

Cells
We have about 40 trillion cells in our bodies—that's 40,000,000,000,000! You can fit 8,000 of these cells on the head of a pin.

Chromosomes
Your genome is shared out into separate packages, called chromosomes. Humans have 23 different chromosomes. There are two copies of each, so that's 46 in total.

Nucleus
The nucleus is the command center of the cell because it contains your genome.

DNA
Surprisingly, 98 percent of DNA isn't used for genes! Scientists haven't yet worked out exactly what it all does.

Are there cells without DNA?

Unusually, red blood cells that carry oxygen around your body don't have a DNA-containing nucleus. They live for only four months and have to be constantly replaced.

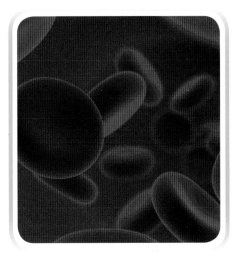

DNA in food

Most of our food comes from living things. When you eat a tomato, for example, you're also eating all of the DNA in its cells. Your body chops up this DNA during digestion.

ANIMAL CELL

IS ALL OUR DNA IN THE NUCLEUS?

No! Some of our DNA lives outside the nucleus in mitochondria, which are tiny batteries that power cells. Plant cells also have DNA inside their chloroplasts, which they use to change sunlight into food.

Mitochondria
There are lots of mitochondria in animal cells, but only one nucleus.

Chloroplasts
Plant cells have chloroplasts, which contain a chemical that makes them green.

PLANT CELL

9

What does **DNA do?**

DNA is a code that makes all life on Earth—from humans to fish, and daffodils to dinosaurs. The main purpose of the DNA code is to make proteins. All living things use proteins to make and repair themselves.

Different codes

Living things on Earth vary a lot because of differences in their DNA code.

FUNGI

Mushrooms, molds, and yeasts are all fungi. Most fungi feed on the remains of dead plants and animals.

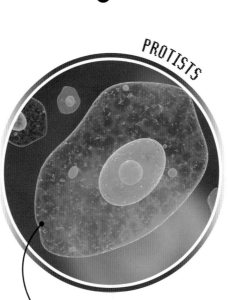

PROTISTS

Protists are single-celled organisms. They contain a nucleus, like the cells of fungi, plants, and animals.

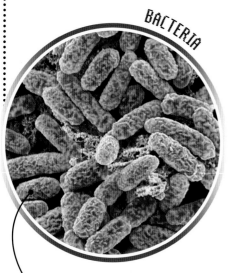

BACTERIA

Bacteria are single-celled, microscopic organisms without a nucleus, but they still have DNA.

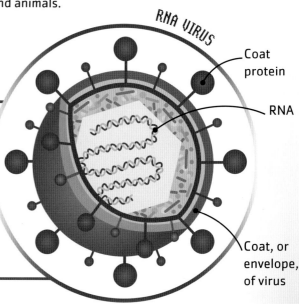

RNA VIRUS

Coat protein

RNA

Coat, or envelope, of virus

WHERE DID DNA COME FROM?

DNA probably developed from a molecule called RNA, which may have made up life billions of years ago. RNA looks a bit like DNA and can also do some of the things that proteins do. Some viruses still use RNA to encode their genes.

There are about 400,000 different species of plant. Most of them are green.

PLANTS

ANIMALS

There are more than a million known species of animal, with many new ones discovered each year!

I'm NOT boring!

IS DNA BORING?

Even after the discovery of DNA, scientists thought it was boring for a long time. This was because DNA is made of only three things: sugar, phosphate, and bases. People thought that it was too simple to hold the code for life.

Inheritance

Before the discovery of DNA, people were puzzled about how certain characteristics were passed on to the next generation. They set out to find a molecule that could be passed on, or **inherited**. People thought the molecule would be a protein— but they were wrong!

Smooth bacterium   DNA   Rough bacterium   Smooth bacterium

DNA can change characteristics

In 1944, scientists discovered that if DNA from smooth bacteria was mixed with rough bacteria, the rough bacteria became smooth. Only DNA could pass on this characteristic, not proteins. This was the proof that DNA was the important stuff!

Characteristics, such as fur color, are passed on from parents to offspring.

11

Let's experiment!

Would you like to try and see DNA for yourself? Perform this fun experiment, which you can do at home. You'll be getting DNA out of strawberries.

YOU WILL NEED

» 2 beakers or plastic cups
» 2 tsp dishwashing liquid
» 1 tsp salt
» ½ cup water
» 2 strawberries
» 1 resealable plastic bag
» Strainer or coffee filter
» ½ cup cold rubbing alcohol
» Tweezers
» 1 scientist (that's you!)

1 Preparing the DNA-extraction mixture
In a beaker, mix together 2 teaspoons of dishwashing liquid, 1 teaspoon of salt, and ½ cup of water.

2 Breaking open the cells
Put the strawberries into the plastic bag, seal the bag, and crush the berries well with your fingers. Add 2 teaspoons of the DNA-extraction mixture, reseal the bag, and continue crushing for another minute.

Don't eat these!

Can I see DNA?

It's very hard to know what something is like **unless you can see it**. DNA is very tiny and hidden in our cells, but we have some tricks for getting it out and taking a look at it!

3 Separating the DNA

Strain the strawberry liquid into the other clean beaker. Next, **gently** add the rubbing alcohol, pouring it down the side of the beaker. Use an amount equal to the amount of strawberry liquid. **DO NOT** mix or stir.

4 Seeing the DNA

Look for a white, cloudy layer at the top of the mixture. You can tilt the cup and pick up this layer using the tweezers. That's the DNA!

DNA

Wow!

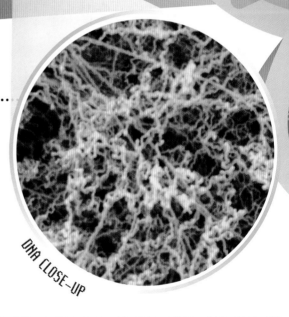

DNA CLOSE-UP

Seeing chromosomes

It's often hard to see DNA in cells because the chromosomes are all spread out. When cells get ready to divide, however, the chromosomes pack up and copy themselves (see **Copying your DNA**, page 24).

UNDER THE MICROSCOPE

We still haven't seen the DNA in much detail, have we? Very powerful microscopes can help us here...

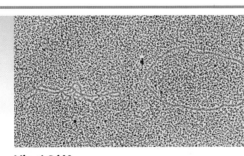

Viral DNA
An electron microscope uses a beam of incredibly tiny particles to show microscopic objects, such as this DNA (blue) from a virus.

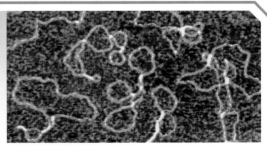

Bacterial DNA
This DNA (pink) from a bacterium has been made visible by an atomic force microscope, which builds up an image of the DNA by probing it with a minute instrument.

The story of DNA

We've seen DNA down the microscope, but we still can't see its **double-helix shape**! How did scientists figure out exactly what it looked like? Well, they had to take a very special kind of **X-ray picture**...

The genius of Franklin and Wilkins

Scientists Maurice Wilkins and Rosalind Franklin had the brilliant idea of firing X-rays at crystals of DNA to find out more about its structure.

WILKINS

FRANKLIN

When you shine a light through a crystal, such as a diamond, the light scatters to reveal a pattern. Franklin bounced X-rays off her DNA crystal and took a photograph of the pattern made by the scattered X-rays. She called this *Photo 51*, and it's the most famous photograph of DNA in the world.

That's me?!!

PHOTO 51

Photo 51 still doesn't look like DNA as we know it! Luckily, Rosalind Franklin was very good at math, and she was able to use complicated equations to reveal the double-helix structure from the X-ray pattern.

When James Watson and Francis Crick saw *Photo 51* and Franklin's math, they realized the importance of what she had discovered. This allowed them to build the first model of the double-helix structure of DNA, in 1953.

This is it!

We've discovered the secret of life!

CRICK

WATSON

Nobel Prize
Watson, Crick, and Wilkins were awarded a Nobel Prize in 1962. Franklin had died four years earlier, so, unfortunately, she didn't get the recognition she deserved.

Hold on... this shape means DNA can copy itself

If you unzip the two sides of the DNA helix, each side can act as a template, or guide, to make a new copy. By matching up new bases to the original strand, you can make two identical DNA double helixes.

Scientists knew that DNA could be passed on to other cells and offspring when cells divide. Now they understood how!

New bases are added to the original strand.

Meet the molecules

Molecules are groups of elements, such as carbon and oxygen, bonded together. DNA is a **big molecule**. To use DNA, you need the help of more molecules, including **RNA** and **proteins**.

RNA

DNA

The DNA molecule looks like a ladder twisted into a spiral—a shape known as a double helix. The double helix is made up of two strands held together by chemicals called bases. These strands form the rungs of the ladder.

DNA DOUBLE HELIX

RNA

Ribo**n**ucleic **a**cid (RNA) is very similar to DNA, but it is only half of a double helix. It's used to make a temporary copy of the DNA sequence when a gene is used (see **Using genes**, page 20).

PROTEIN

Proteins

DNA is the instruction manual of the cell, but proteins do all the work! Proteins allow cells to do all the things they need to do to keep our bodies working. They often act as tiny—but very complicated—machines.

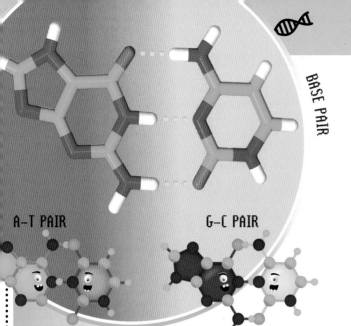

BASE PAIR

A-T PAIR

G-C PAIR

Chromosomes

Each chromosome contains one continuous molecule of DNA. Our biggest chromosome is 249,956,422 bases (A, T, C, G) long. If you were to write all the letters out in a book like this, you'd need 16,597 books just for that one chromosome!

Bases

The bases in the rungs of the DNA ladder come in four types and spell out the DNA code. There is adenine (A), which pairs with thymine (T) in the double helix, and cytosine (C), which pairs with guanine (G).

CHROMOSOMES

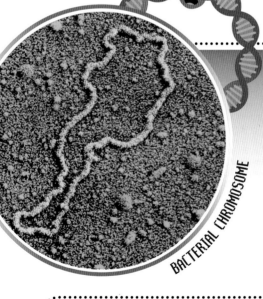

Chromosomes in bacteria

Bacteria have just one chromosome, which is very different from ours. Unlike a human chromosome, it makes a loop or ring and doesn't live inside a nucleus.

BACTERIAL CHROMOSOME

Ribosomes

Ribosomes are tiny factories inside the cell that make proteins. RNA copies of genes are delivered to ribosomes. There, they are decoded to make the correct protein.

RIBOSOME

Human chromosomes

If you were to spread out all of your chromosomes from one nucleus in your body, they would look something like this. Humans have **23** pairs of chromosomes, 46 in total. One chromosome in each of the pairs comes from **each** of your biological parents.

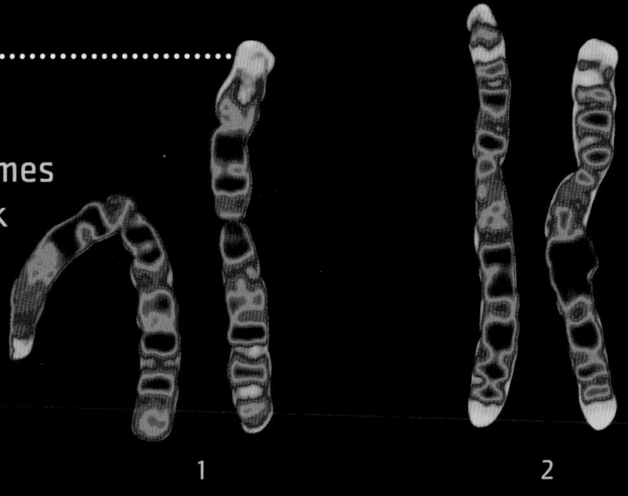

1

2

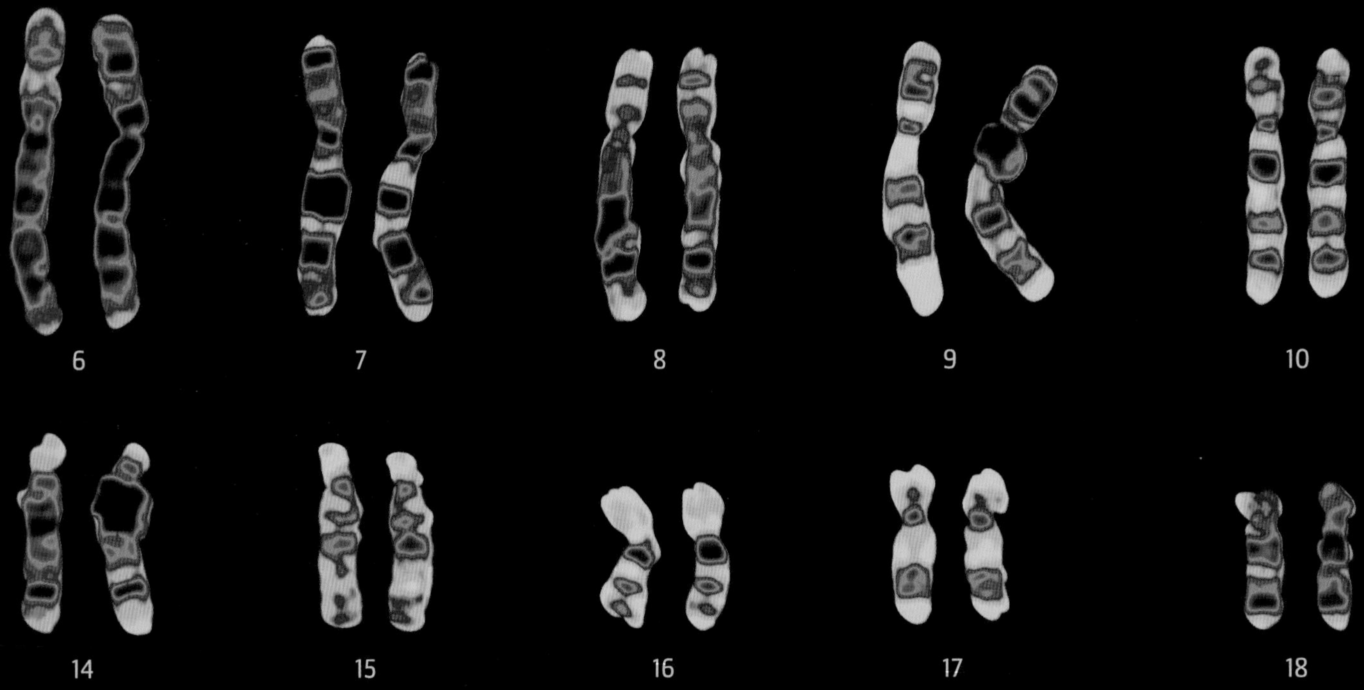

6

7

8

9

10

14

15

16

17

18

What are
chromosomes?

Chromosomes contain DNA, and they keep all the genetic information safe. Different organisms have **different numbers** of chromosomes. We have 46 chromosomes, guinea pigs have 64, and chimps have 48—the same number as potatoes!

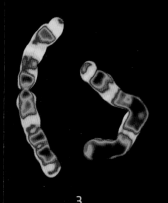
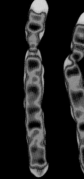
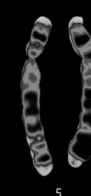

3

4

5

11

12

13

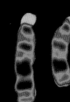

19

20

21

22

Chromosome pair 23 consists of the sex chromosomes. There are two types, called X and Y. These are special because they help to determine whether you are male or female.

X X

Usually, **girls** have **two X** chromosomes and **boys** have **one X** and **one Y**.

CRAZY CHROMOSOMES

The number of chromosomes in living things varies hugely and can be surprising. An elephant has 56 chromosomes, but a chicken has 78!

Jumper ants
These poisonous Australian ants only have one pair of chromosomes. Common garden ants have 15 pairs.

Adder's tongue fern
Perhaps surprisingly, plants often have lots of chromosomes. The adder's tongue fern has 1,262 chromosomes—that's the most found so far in any living thing!

Atlas blue butterfly
This butterfly from North Africa has 452 chromosomes. That's the largest-known number of chromosomes in an animal.

Transcription

When a protein needs to be made, the gene that makes it must be activated. This process is called **transcription**. DNA can't leave the nucleus of the cell, so instead, a temporary copy of the DNA code is transcribed into a molecule of messenger RNA (mRNA), which can leave the nucleus.

1 **Genes**
The DNA code is made up of many genes. Genes are only read once they get a "go" signal from the cell.

GENE

GENE

INSULIN PROTEIN

Genes make proteins

Each gene usually contains the instructions for making one protein. Proteins come in different shapes and sizes and do all the work in your cells. Some of them, such as insulin, are important hormones that travel around your body in the blood.

Using genes

Your DNA code is like an instruction manual made up of lots of different sentences, called **genes**. When you need to use a gene, its code is read. Each gene is marked with a **start** and a **stop** code, like a capital letter and a period in a sentence.

② Gene unwinds

Once your gene gets the "go" signal, its DNA unwinds. This separates the base pairs so that a copy can be made.

③ mRNA is made

A single-stranded copy of the gene sequence is made using RNA bases. These make an mRNA molecule that can be destroyed once the required protein has been made.

The mRNA strand ends when it reaches a **stop** code.

mRNA

One difference between RNA and DNA is that RNA uses the base uracil (U) instead of thymine (T).

GENE

④ DNA winds back up

After the mRNA copy of the code has been made, the DNA is wound back up again to keep the information safe. Any damage could result in a **mutation**.

MEMBRANE OF NUCLEUS

⑤

Leaving the nucleus

Now we have mRNA, but we still need to read it. For this to happen, the mRNA leaves the nucleus through a pore (hole).

NUCLEUS

6

Codons
Each group of three letters makes up a single word in the gene, called a codon.

tRNA molecule

AMINO ACID

AMINO ACID

AMINO ACID

G A U A G A U G A U C U A C U

Reading the code
The ribosome is incredibly fast at translating the mRNA sequence into protein. It can join up amino acids at a rate of 200 per minute. The biggest protein in the human body is called titin, and it takes almost three hours to make.

7

Amino acids and tRNA
Each codon codes for an amino acid and each amino acid is attached to a tRNA molecule. These pair with the codons on the mRNA.

Cracking **the code**

Can you read the instructions written in the genetic code? No? Well, you'll need the help of a type of RNA called **transfer RNA (tRNA)** and a **ribosome**. They form a team that cracks the code and follows its instructions to make **proteins**.

Ribosome

The ribosome is a hard-working molecular machine. It matches the codons in the mRNA to tRNA, which brings in the amino acids needed to make proteins. This process is called **translation**.

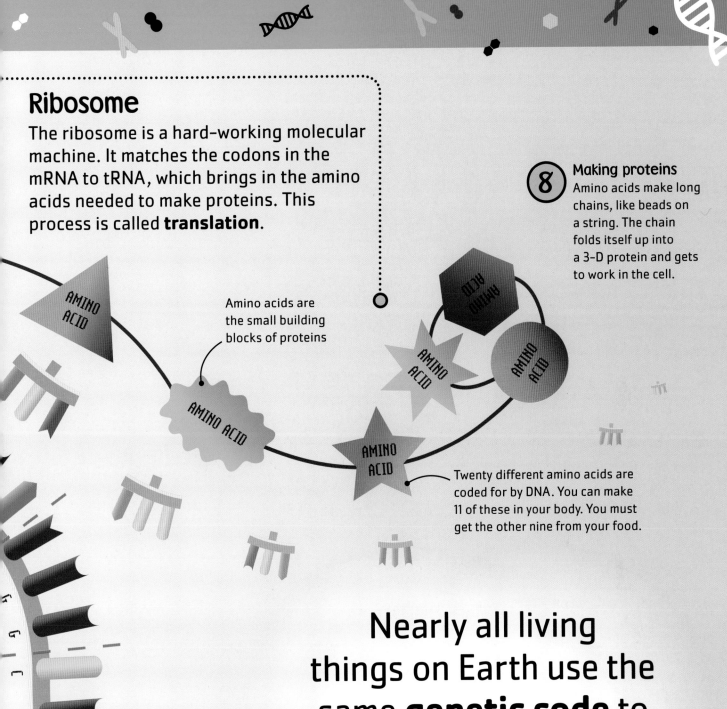

8 **Making proteins**
Amino acids make long chains, like beads on a string. The chain folds itself up into a 3-D protein and gets to work in the cell.

Amino acids are the small building blocks of proteins

AMINO ACID

AMINO ACID

AMINO ACID

AMINO ACID

AMINO ACID

AMINO ACID

Twenty different amino acids are coded for by DNA. You can make 11 of these in your body. You must get the other nine from your food.

Nearly all living things on Earth use the same **genetic code** to make proteins from the same **animo acids**.

Copying your DNA

A complete copy of your DNA is inside nearly every one of the **40 trillion cells** in your body. Each time your body makes a new cell, you need to **replicate**, or make a copy of, all your DNA so that the new cell knows what to do.

A human skin cell divides in two to form two daughter cells. Grown in a lab, these cells can help scientists learn about wound healing.

DNA replication

When DNA copies itself, it first unwinds into two separate strands. Then, a special protein called a **DNA polymerase** matches new DNA bases with the sequence on the two unwound halves of the helix. This completes the two new DNA strands.

DNA polymerase

The two strands are copied in opposite directions.

Newly added base

Each day, you make
330 billion feet
(100 billion meters) of DNA!

Why do we need new cells?

Whenever you grow or repair any damage, such as a cut, you need new cells. New cells are made by **cell division**. Before a cell can divide, it first needs to copy all of its DNA. The "parent" cell then splits in two, making two new "daughter" cells, each with a complete set of DNA.

It's time to split!

STAGE 1

Copying chromosomes
Each chromosome replicates itself to form two strands of DNA, which are stuck to each other in the middle. The membrane of the nucleus then breaks down.

STAGE 2

Lining up
The replicated chromosomes attach to threadlike fibers that help them line up in the center of the cell.

STAGE 3

Pulled apart
Pulling from the fibers separates the two halves of the replicated chromosomes. The two copies move into different halves of the cell as the cell begins to divide.

STAGE 4

Daughter cells
The parent cell will now become two daughter cells, each with a complete copy of DNA in a newly formed nucleus.

Do all your cells have the same DNA?

Scientists used to think that cells became **specialized** for a particular role in the body by losing part of their DNA. We now know that different cell types contain the same DNA, **so why do they look so different**?

Heart muscle cells

The muscles in your arms and legs need to rest after use. However, heart muscle is different. It never rests and keeps working every moment until you die.

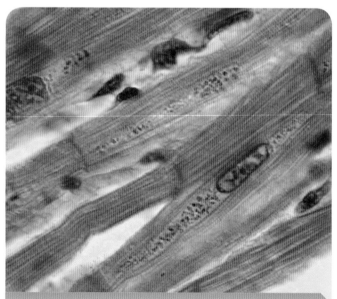

FACT FILE

» Heart cells beat by themselves, even when they are grown in a Petri dish!

» Heart cells are full of mitochondria to give them lots of energy.

» Your heart beats 100,000 times a day.

Neurons

Neurons, or nerve cells, are very long cells that transmit signals in and out of your brain and spine. These signals travel as fast as 250 mph (400 kph)!

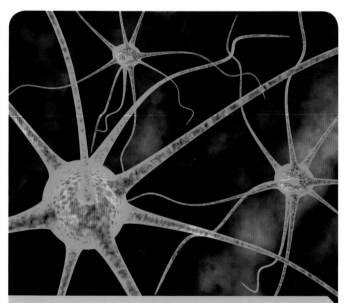

FACT FILE

» Our brains contain about 86 billion neurons.

» Your longest neuron is 3 ft 4 in (1 m) long, from your spine to your toes.

» Giraffes have neurons that are more than 16 ft 6 in (5 m) long!

DIFFERENT CELLS, DIFFERENT GENES

Your whole genome is not active in every cell. Instead, different cells just use the genes they need. In a heart muscle cell, only the genes that are needed to make and run heart muscle are active. Other specialized genes that make different cells, such as neurons, are tightly locked away and can't be read.

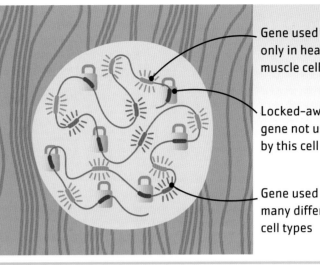

Gene used only in heart muscle cells

Locked-away gene not used by this cell type

Gene used by many different cell types

Bone cells

The outside of your bones is made up of a hard tissue filled with long-lasting, star-shaped cells that help take care of the bones.

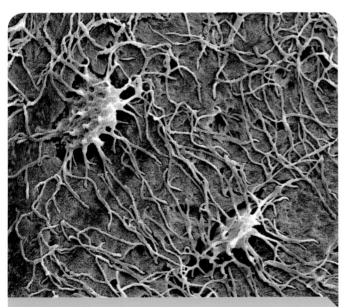

FACT FILE

» Bones also store minerals inside your body.

» The smallest bone in your body is in your ear and helps you hear.

» Birds have lightweight, hollow bones to help them fly.

Lung cells

The lining of your lungs is made up of cells that allow oxygen from the air into your blood—and carbon dioxide out— when you breathe.

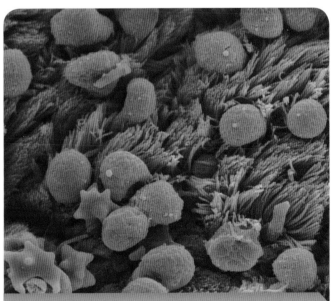

FACT FILE

» Lung cells are covered with little brushlike structures to sweep out gunk.

» The total surface area inside both of your lungs is about the size of a tennis court!

» Lungs have 1,500 miles (2,400 km) of airways.

Passing on your genes

Living things **pass on** their genes to the **next generation**. This means that children often look like their parents, since they share half of their genes with their mother and half with their father. This is called **genetic inheritance**.

Cocker spaniel mom sheds her hair.

Two versions of every gene

The cockerpoo puppies here have two copies of each of their chromosomes—one from Mom and one from Dad. This means that they, just like humans and many other animals, have two versions of every gene. Different versions of the same gene are called **alleles** (a–leelz).

Inheritance
Each puppy has inherited its own mix of genes from its parents.

DOMINANT ALLELES

If you have two alleles of the same gene, such as the gene that controls hair-shedding, which one wins? Some alleles are dominant—their instructions override other alleles—and they always win.

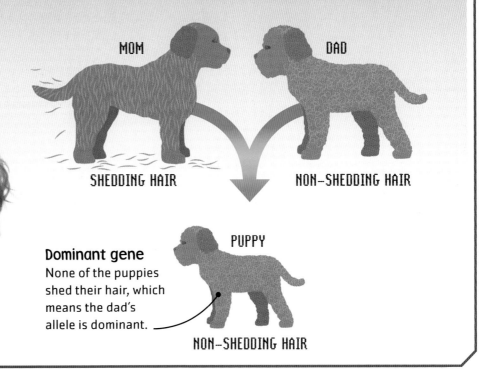

MOM

DAD

SHEDDING HAIR

NON-SHEDDING HAIR

Dominant gene
None of the puppies shed their hair, which means the dad's allele is dominant.

PUPPY

NON-SHEDDING HAIR

Poodle dad has non-shedding hair.

Non-shedding hair
All the puppies have non-shedding hair because of their poodle dad's dominant gene.

Scientists can **compare the DNA** of different dog breeds to find out which **genes code** for which characteristics.

Everyone's a
mutant

Unlike a printed book, genomes can change. Changes in the DNA sequence can happen when there's a **mistake** in copying it. These changes are called **mutations**. Because our DNA sequences are all a bit different, **we are actually all mutants**.

We're all different!

Humans share a lot of their DNA code with one another. However, we all have about 3 million differences from one another, too. Mutations happen in every generation—you have about 60 new mutations that are unique to just you.

Siamese fur

Siamese cats have a mutation in a gene that makes the black pigment in their fur break down easily. This means that the color gets destroyed when it warms up. It survives only in the cat's cooler body parts, such as its nose, ears, and paws!

DNA polymerase, which copies your DNA, is **very accurate**—it makes just one mistake every **10 billion** base pairs.

Quickly draw a picture of a cat. Give yourself 30 seconds to copy it. Cover your first drawing and give yourself another 30 seconds to copy your second drawing.

Copycats
How similar are your cats? You'll probably see a few differences. You have created mutants!

Good mutations

Mutations **change genes**, and genes control almost everything about who you are! Mutations **happen randomly** and can be good or bad for you—they might make you stronger or weaker, taller or shorter, or even give you a **special new skill**, such as the ability to see in the dark!

Natural selection

Good, or useful, mutations increase the chances that creatures will have their own babies and so pass on the good mutations. This process is called **natural selection**.

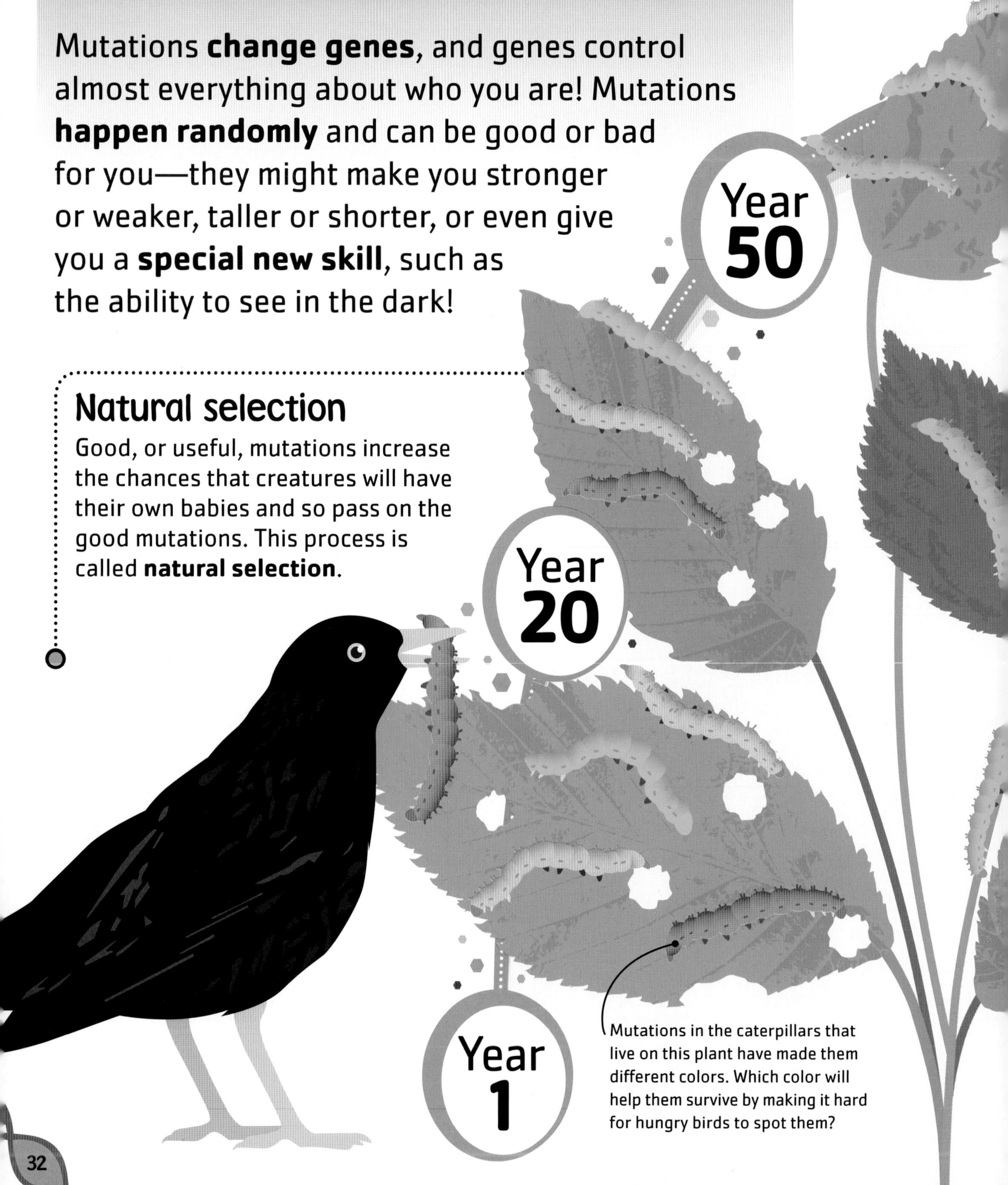

Year
50

Year
20

Year
1

Mutations in the caterpillars that live on this plant have made them different colors. Which color will help them survive by making it hard for hungry birds to spot them?

Green mutants can hide on the green plant so they don't get eaten as often. They are more likely to live long enough to have babies and pass on their green genes.

Year 100

What new **biological superpower** would you like?

Year 1,000

There are now only green caterpillars. Natural selection has taken place, and the green mutation, or allele, has triumphed.

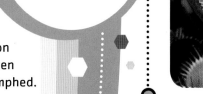

Natural selection in action

We can see beautiful examples of natural selection all around us on Earth. Passing on useful mutations makes species better able to survive in the places they live.

Giraffes
These magnificent mammals are adapted, or suited, to eating leaves high up in trees. They keep and pass on genes that help make long necks.

Polar bears
Polar bears are experts in camouflage. They have selected white fur genes to help them hide in the snow, unlike other bears.

Pufferfish
These fish have adapted to puff themselves up so that they look scary to enemies. They are also spiked and poisonous!

Penguins
Penguins have lots of adaptations! They are waterproof, use fat to keep warm, and have given up flying to become expert swimmers.

Venus flytrap
This plant lives in soil low in nutrients. It has evolved special leaves that snap shut to catch insects. Once trapped, the unlucky insect is digested by the plant.

Evolution

Natural selection, in which good mutations are passed on, changes living things and can lead to **brand new species**! This is called **evolution**, and it usually happens slowly, over millions of years.

Charles Darwin
In 1831, the scientist Charles Darwin sailed to South America. On his voyage, he saw lots of weird animals and plants that he'd never seen before. He started to wonder where they all came from.

Darwin's finches

Darwin realized that the different types of finch on the Galápagos Islands were all related. However, they had differently shaped beaks, depending on where they lived on the islands. Each beak had become specially adapted for, or suited to, eating different kinds of food.

Changing beak
Since Darwin, this finch's diet has changed from soft seeds to larger, harder ones. To cope with this, its beak has evolved to become bigger!

LARGE GROUND FINCH

MEDIUM GROUND FINCH

FACT FILE
» Scientific name: *Geospiza magnirostris*
» Beak: Bulky and powerful
» Diet: Large nuts and seeds

FACT FILE
» Scientific name: *Geospiza fortis*
» Beak: Strong and deep
» Diet: Seeds

A voyage of discovery

Darwin's voyage, aboard a ship called HMS *Beagle*, took him to the Galápagos Islands, west of South America. Based on what he saw, Darwin realized that all life on Earth must be connected. He wrote about his ideas in a book called *On the Origin of Species*.

Galápagos Islands

GALÁPAGOS ISLANDS

N
W · E
S

Darwin's ship
HMS *Beagle* sailed to South America to plot maps. The ship's captain, Robert FitzRoy, took Darwin to study wildlife.

SMALL TREE FINCH

GREEN WARBLER-FINCH

FACT FILE
» Scientific name: *Camarhynchus parvulus*
» Beak: Small and sharp
» Diet: Insects

FACT FILE
» Scientific name: *Certhidea olivacea*
» Beak: Pointed for foraging under bark
» Diet: Small insects and spiders

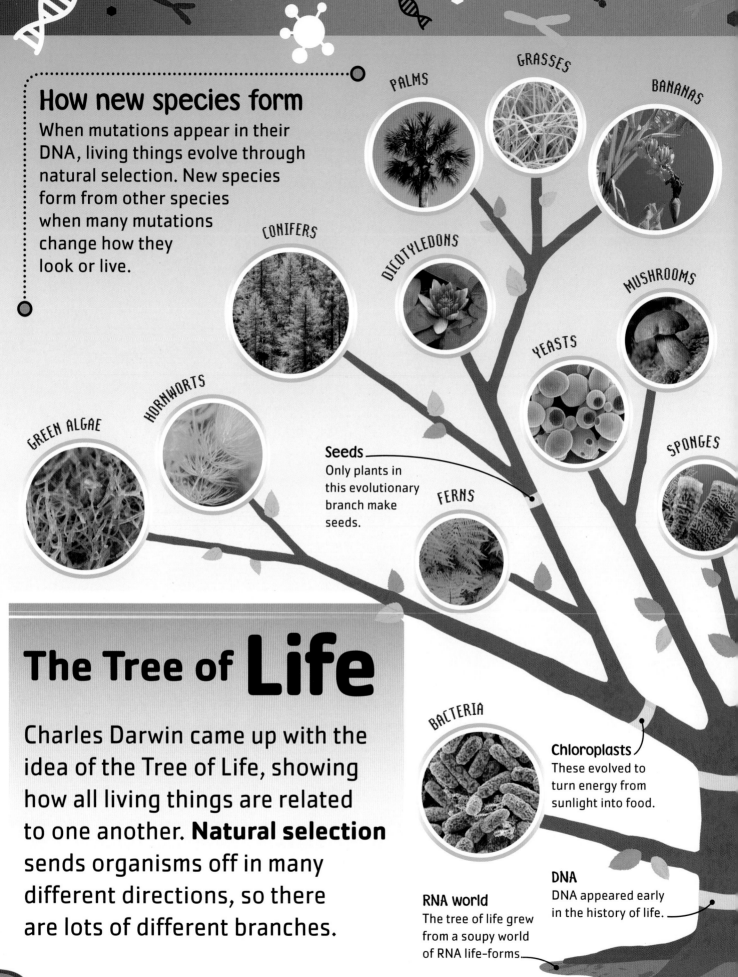

How new species form

When mutations appear in their DNA, living things evolve through natural selection. New species form from other species when many mutations change how they look or live.

PALMS

GRASSES

BANANAS

CONIFERS

DICOTYLEDONS

MUSHROOMS

YEASTS

HORNWORTS

GREEN ALGAE

Seeds
Only plants in this evolutionary branch make seeds.

FERNS

SPONGES

The Tree of Life

Charles Darwin came up with the idea of the Tree of Life, showing how all living things are related to one another. **Natural selection** sends organisms off in many different directions, so there are lots of different branches.

BACTERIA

Chloroplasts
These evolved to turn energy from sunlight into food.

DNA
DNA appeared early in the history of life.

RNA world
The tree of life grew from a soupy world of RNA life-forms.

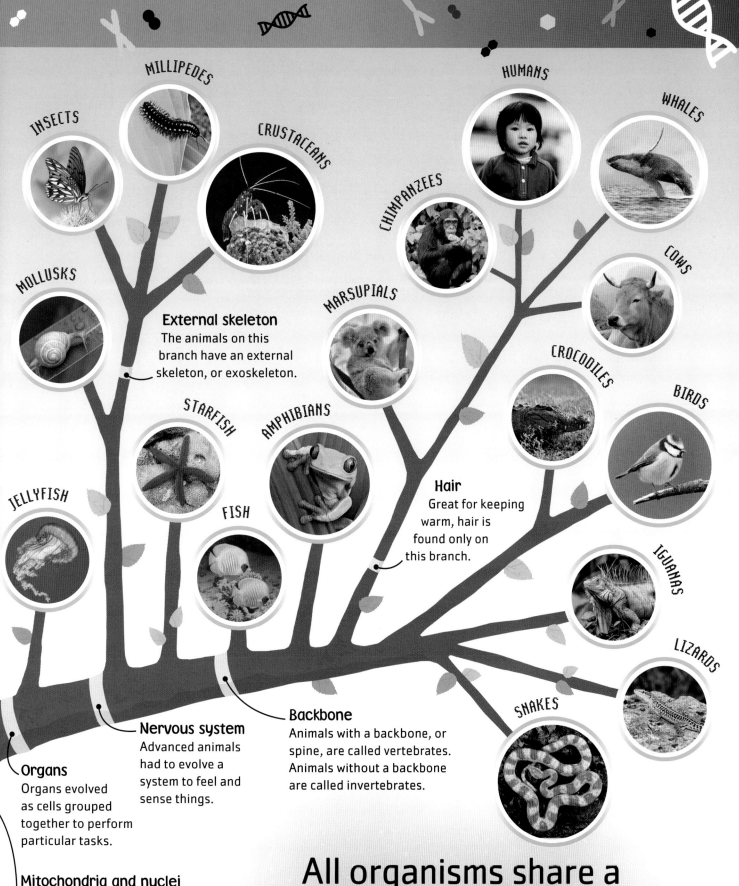

INSECTS

MILLIPEDES

CRUSTACEANS

HUMANS

WHALES

CHIMPANZEES

COWS

MOLLUSKS

MARSUPIALS

External skeleton
The animals on this branch have an external skeleton, or exoskeleton.

CROCODILES

BIRDS

STARFISH

AMPHIBIANS

JELLYFISH

FISH

Hair
Great for keeping warm, hair is found only on this branch.

IGUANAS

LIZARDS

SNAKES

Nervous system
Advanced animals had to evolve a system to feel and sense things.

Backbone
Animals with a backbone, or spine, are called vertebrates. Animals without a backbone are called invertebrates.

Organs
Organs evolved as cells grouped together to perform particular tasks.

Mitochondria and nuclei
Some early cells evolved mitochondria, to give them energy, and a nucleus.

All organisms share a common ancestor that lived **four billion years ago.**

Primates are closely related to rodents, such as mice. We shared an ancestor about 80 million years ago, and we have the same mammal characteristics, such as hair.

COW
80%

Cows and humans are both mammals. We both have bony skeletons and hair and we breathe air, but we look very different.

MOUSE
80%

CAT
90%

Cats have 19 pairs of chromosomes in their cells, whereas humans have 23 pairs. Many of the genes on them are the same though.

Shared genes

Some genes are so similar between different species that they can be swapped around by scientists and still work. Human genes can even work in the fungus yeast!

CHIMPANZEE
96%
SIMILAR TO HUMANS

One of our closest living relatives is the chimpanzee. We are both primates, and we have a common ancestor who lived about five million years ago.

FRUIT FLY 60%

We don't share as many genes with insects as we do with vertebrates. However, some genes, such as the ones that put your head, body, and legs in the right order, are similar.

THAT'S BANANAS

We share 50 percent of our genes with bananas! All animals and plants share a common ancestor—a single-celled life-form that lived more than a billion years ago. Many of the chemical processes that organisms need to survive are the same, so the genes that code for them are very similar.

We are family?

We like to think that as a species **humans** are unique, but, actually, we **share a lot of genes** with other animals. In fact, we are more closely related to some species of apes than they are to each other!

All humans are

99.9%

genetically similar.

Humans are related to all living things, but we are most closely related to each other. All the things that make each person different, such as eye color, are due to differences in just 0.1 percent of our genes.

Model organisms

Living things that are very easy to study in a laboratory are called **model organisms**. Here are some on these laboratory shelves! They're like a collection of useful creatures that helps us understand how biology works.

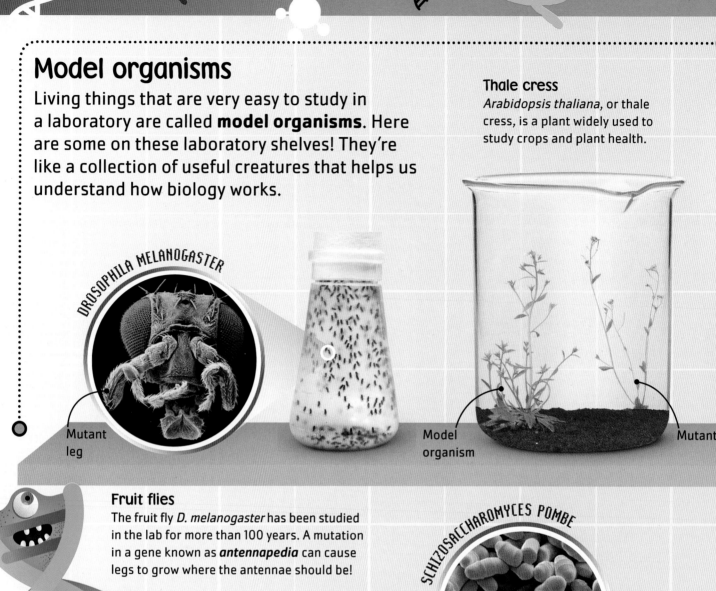

Thale cress

Arabidopsis thaliana, or thale cress, is a plant widely used to study crops and plant health.

DROSOPHILA MELANOGASTER

Mutant leg

Model organism

Mutant

Fruit flies

The fruit fly *D. melanogaster* has been studied in the lab for more than 100 years. A mutation in a gene known as *antennapedia* can cause legs to grow where the antennae should be!

SCHIZOSACCHAROMYCES POMBE

Learning from
each other

We share a lot of our DNA with other living things. So, if we can understand how a gene works in another animal, plant, or even a fungus, we can get a good idea of how that gene might work in us.

Fission yeast

Scientists have learned a lot about how cells divide by studying this yeast (*S. pombe*). It has a mutant form that keeps growing but can't divide!

C. elegans worms have only **959** body cells.

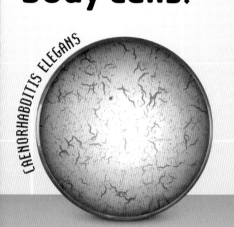

CAENORHABDITIS ELEGANS

GFP
The jellyfish gene makes a glow-in-the-dark protein called **green fluorescent protein** (GFP). The protein glows when you shine ultraviolet light on it.

Jellyfish
GFP was isolated from the glow-in-the-dark jellyfish *Aequorea victoria*.

Nematode worm
C. elegans is a tiny—just 0.04 in (1 mm) long—nematode worm that lives in rotting fruit. It is used to study lots of biological processes.

Gene with attached GFP is active in neurons.

See-through
Nematodes are transparent, and so it is easy to see which cells glow with GFP.

Model organism

Mutant mouse

Mice
Mice (*Mus musculus*) are very useful because they are mammals, like us. We know from studies on mice that you need a gene that makes a protein called leptin to store fat properly. Mice with a faulty leptin gene get very fat.

Jellyfish gene
Jellyfish have a gene that lets them glow in the dark. Scientists can borrow this gene and attach it to genes in other animals, such as the nematode *C. elegans*. When the gene being studied is active, scientists can see which cells it affects because they will glow.

Bad
mutations

Mutations that **change DNA sequences** can stop genes from working properly. This may mean that a protein **can't be made** or, if it can still be made, it **doesn't work**.

PUG

Mutations in pets

Humans like to create breeds of pets with characteristics that they find attractive. This **selective breeding** means that some pets have mutations that make them less healthy compared to their wild relatives. Is it right to keep these breeds going?

ALBINO HEDGEHOG

HAIRLESS RAT

Breathing difficulties
People find pugs' flat faces cute, but their squashed noses often cause them breathing problems.

Easy prey
Albino animals don't produce any colored pigments. They are spotted more easily by predators and are at risk of sunburn.

Feeling cold
Hair is important in the wild for warmth, protection, and camouflage. Hairless pets need to be kept warm or they will suffer.

COLOR-BLINDNESS

Color-blindness means that you can't see different colors, as in the test picture (right). People with the most common type, called red-green color-blindness, can't see the green squiggly line. This condition is more common in boys than girls.

COLOR-BLINDNESS TEST

SCOTTISH FOLD

DWARF RABBIT

SILKIE CHICKEN

Joint problems
These cats have mutant cartilage that folds their ears. It also causes severe arthritis—pain, stiffness, and swelling in the joints.

Deadly double
The mutation in dwarf rabbits makes them very small. However, if a baby rabbit inherits two copies of the mutant gene, it won't survive.

Fluff, not feathers!
This breed's mutant fluffy feathers are not waterproof and are useless for flight. Silkies also have a gap in their skulls that makes their heads fragile.

Faulty genes in us

If a mutation **alters the DNA sequence** of your genes, this tiny change can sometimes cause **big problems** for the cells in your body. This is called a **genetic disorder**.

Point mutations

A change of just one DNA base is called a **point mutation**, and it can cause a genetic disorder, such as **cystic fibrosis**. In this disorder, cells that line the lungs don't work properly, and the lungs get clogged with thick, sticky mucus.

DNA sequence in a healthy gene
This sequence of DNA bases is from a healthy gene that makes a functioning protein.

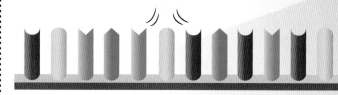

DNA sequence with a point mutation
Just one change in the DNA sequence may have a big effect. It might stop a gene from making a protein, or cause the gene to make a protein that doesn't work properly in the body. Mutations are inherited in families when they are copied into eggs or sperm.

IMMUNE CELLS ATTACKING A CANCER CELL

Cancer

Cancer is a genetic disorder caused by DNA mutations. However, it is only passed on through families when the cells with the cancer-causing mutations make sperm or eggs—which is rare.

White blood cells

A part of our immune system, white blood cells act like soldiers, finding and attacking enemy cells, including cancer cells.

Cancer cell

Some cancer cells can hide from white blood cells. However, new cancer drugs can boost the immune system and help find and fight the cancer.

Causes of mutations

Mutations can be caused by energy absorbed into cells, as well as by errors in DNA replication. Strong sunlight on skin cells may lead to mutations.

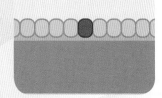

Uncontrolled growth

Mutations can cause cell division to go out of control, producing too many cells in one place. These extra cells form masses, called tumors.

Invasion

Cancerous tumors can invade other tissues and spread around the body. They stop it from working normally and can make you very sick.

SICKLE CELL ANEMIA

Two copies of a bad sickle-cell mutation cause red blood cells to change their shape and block blood vessels (tubes in your body that carry blood). However, one mutant version of the gene, together with a healthy copy, protects you against the disease malaria!

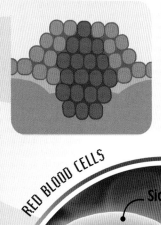

RED BLOOD CELLS

Sickle cell

Normal, round red blood cell

Sequencing DNA

There are about 3,000,000,000 bases in the human genome, and, by 2003, scientists had determined their precise order. Due to amazing advances in technology, we can now find out the **DNA sequence** of any organism on Earth!

Sanger sequencing

Fred Sanger invented a method to read DNA sequences one base at a time. He used the process of DNA replication itself to do this. Sanger is one of only a handful of scientists to have won two Nobel Prizes!

 1 The DNA and all the molecules needed to copy the DNA, including spare G, C, A, and T bases, are put into four different test tubes. Faulty G, C, A, or T bases are added to each test tube.

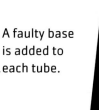 A faulty base is added to each tube.

 2 The copying process is started. If the DNA replication machinery inserts a faulty base, the chain stops. This is called **chain termination**.

A faulty G stops the copying.

3 It's completely random where the faulty bases get inserted. So if you make enough copies, then all possible chain lengths will be made in each tube, all ending in that particular base.

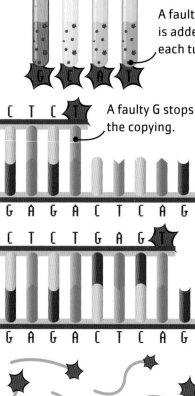

 4 At the end of the experiment, lots of different lengths of DNA will have been made, all representing each time that particular base (G, C, A, or T) appears in the sequence.

 5 Time to sort all the lengths of DNA out in each tube according to size. This is done using a DNA gel.

Pieces of DNA travel in an electric current from the top of the gel to the bottom. Short pieces move farther and faster than long pieces, so are found at the bottom of the gel.

C   A   T

CAN YOU READ THE CODE?
Use a ruler to help you read the sequence of the DNA in the gel. Start at the bottom with the shortest piece of DNA (clue: it's an A) and slide the ruler up to find the next band. Is it G, C, or T? Write each letter down as you move upward. (For the answer, see the bottom of the opposite page.)

To sequence lots of DNA, faster and cheaper technology is now available, like this minION, which connects straight to your computer!

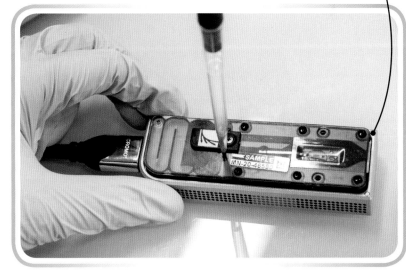

Sequencing genomes today

Technology has advanced incredibly quickly in the last few years. We can now sequence a genome as complicated as ours in just a few hours.

THE HUMAN GENOME PROJECT

In 2003, the whole of the human genome was sequenced for the first time using Fred Sanger's invention. This international project involved hundreds of scientists from many countries and took 13 years to complete. It was masterminded by a British scientist named John Sulston.

Hair

The part of hair that you can see is just made up of protein, not cells, so it has no DNA. The follicle—the part of a hair underneath the skin—is made up of cells, so it can be used to create a DNA profile.

Skin cells

Scientists can get a DNA sequence from as few as five skin cells, but it's often best to have more. We shed 400,000 skin cells every day!

Blood

Scientists can extract samples of DNA from cells in blood.

Collecting clues

There may only be a few drops of blood, a few skin cells, or a single hair left at the scene of a crime. However, that's enough to get a sample of DNA.

Hah!

DNA detectives

DNA **evidence** taken from the **scene of a crime** can be very useful in figuring out what happened. Matching DNA samples to suspects can help **catch the criminal**.

CRIME SCENE KIT

It's very important that crime scene evidence isn't mixed up or contaminated. The scientists collecting samples don't want to accidentally test for their own DNA.

Gloves
Gloves stop the scientists from leaving skin cells at the scene.

Swabs
These are used to collect samples of blood and saliva.

Tweezers
Tweezers can be used to pick up samples of hair.

Plastic bags
All samples are kept in sealed bags to stop them from being contaminated.

DNA samples from suspected criminals can be sequenced to produce a **DNA profile**, which can then be matched to DNA evidence from crime scenes. Everyone has a unique DNA sequence, so a specific person can be matched to the evidence.

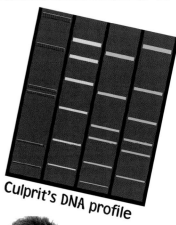

Culprit's DNA profile

Who's the culprit?

Can you match the DNA profile at the top to the person who committed the crime?

Identical twins have very similar DNA, so it's **very hard to tell** which twin has committed a crime just from DNA!

ANSWER: 3

49

Return of the **king**

In August 1485, King Richard III of England was killed at the Battle of Bosworth and buried in Grey Friars Church near Leicester. The church was later demolished and the area eventually became a parking lot. In 2012, **archeologists dug up a skeleton** in the parking lot, which they suspected might belong to the missing king.

Examining the evidence

As with any missing person's case, the investigators brought together lots of strands of evidence to come to a conclusion. It was calculated that there was a 99.999 percent chance that the skeleton was that of Richard III. He was later reburied in Leicester Cathedral.

The skeleton has a curved spine, as Richard was described as having.

THE TOWER OF LONDON

CONSPIRACY!

Many people believe that Richard III killed his two nephews in the Tower of London so that he could become king instead of his older brother's sons.

REPLICA OF RICHARD'S SKELETON

WHAT WE NOW KNOW ABOUT RICHARD III FROM HIS DNA

» There's a 96 percent probability that Richard had **blue eyes**.

» There's a 77 percent chance that he had **blond hair** (which darkened in adulthood).

» The most accurate portrait of Richard is the one we've shown on the opposite page, from the Society of Antiquaries in London.

Mitochondrial DNA

Mitochondrial DNA is special because it only gets passed on through your mother. Therefore, it is identical between siblings. Richard's mitochondrial DNA was passed on by his sister to her daughters and granddaughters through the female line—for 19 generations!

Geneticists compared the mitochondrial DNA sequences and found that they were identical, proving that the skeleton was that of Richard III.

Each peak shows a base.

MICHAEL IBSEN

WENDY DULDIG

THE SKELETON

The skeleton showed signs of injuries suffered on the battlefield where Richard died.

Mitochondrial DNA was found in the skeleton after more than 500 years!

Mike and Wendy
By tracing the family tree, researchers found two living relatives, Mike and Wendy. They had the same mitochondrial DNA sequence as King Richard's skeleton.

Can we
fix genes?

A genetic disorder can be caused by a **mutation in just one gene**. If we can fix this mutation in the cells that use the gene, then we can cure the disease. This is called **gene therapy**.

(1) Faulty cells whose DNA needs to be edited are taken from the patient.

(2) In the lab, a virus is altered genetically so that it can't make you sick.

(3) The healthy version of the gene that has gone wrong in the patient's cells is inserted into the altered virus.

Gene therapy

There are two possible types of gene therapy. **Somatic gene therapy** only treats the patient's diseased cells, but **germ line gene therapy** changes all the cells in the body, including the ones that will be passed on to the next generation.

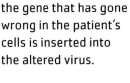

(4) The altered virus containing the healthy DNA "infects" the cells that were removed from the patient.

(5) The cells start to use the gene from the virus to make a healthy protein.

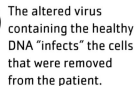

Changing DNA in your **eggs** or **sperm** means that the change will be passed on forever!

6

The altered cells are put back into the patient, and the healthy protein helps cure the disease.

BABY IN A BUBBLE

Gene therapy can cure babies born with a weak immune system. These children can't fight off infections, so they must be kept inside germ-free "bubbles." Now, their cells can be genetically altered to give them an immune system that works, so they can live normally.

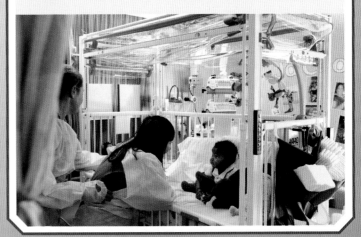

Intelligence could be improved?

If everyone were as intelligent as Albert Einstein, what would life be like?

Who gets access to this technology? Is it only going to be for very rich people?

HUMAN GENES

Human disease could be cured?

You might pass this on to your children.

Should we change genes?

People could be more "beautiful"?

What do you think?

If everyone were changed to be the same, a new disease might evolve that could wipe us all out!

People could be more athletic?

Disease-resistant crops?

Would it taste as nice?

Crops could be altered to make more food from the same number of plants?

Now that we are finding **new ways of altering our genes** and those of other organisms, we don't need to wait for **natural selection** anymore. This means that we can think about making changes for ourselves. But, is it always a good idea to **tinker with genes**?

Would we end up growing fewer varieties of fruits and vegetables?

Bacteria could eat plastic?

Will the change spread into wild populations of the altered species?

PLANT AND BACTERIAL GENES

Plants could cope with drought?

Fruits and vegetables could last longer in stores?

Will it interfere with other plants and animals that live in the same place?

Let's clone plants!

Plants are special because every single cell can grow into a new plant that is a clone of the first plant. You can try cloning lavender yourself!

We're indentical!

 Take a cutting
Cut a fresh, green stem with no flowers from a healthy lavender plant. Remove the leaves at the bottom of the stem so that they don't rot in the soil.

2 **Plant the cutting**
Fill a small plant pot with free-draining compost or soil and plant the lavender cutting firmly in the middle.

3 **Keep moist**
Water the plant well and secure a clear plastic bag over the top of the pot to keep the soil moist. Place it somewhere warm and light.

Rise of the clones!

Cloning is the process of producing genetically identical individuals, with **exactly the same DNA**. Sometimes this happens naturally, as with identical twins. Farmers clone fruit trees to make sure they produce the same tasty fruit, such as apples.

Flowers

Flowers make seeds when they are fertilized by other plants. Plants grown from seeds will not be clones.

APHIDS

CLONING THEMSELVES

A few, very unusual, animals can reproduce by cloning themselves. These female aphids are able to have babies without a male. They produce daughters that are all genetically identical to the mother.

4 **Enjoy the flowers**
After a few weeks, you will see new leaves at the top of your new plant, and eventually flowers. You have created a clone of your original plant!

Cloning animals

In 1996, **Dolly the sheep** was born. Scientists made her by transferring the DNA–containing nucleus of an udder cell into an egg without a nucleus. Dolly was a clone of the mother who gave the nucleus. A whole new sheep was made from an udder cell!

Egg cell
The egg cell has had its nucleus destroyed to remove its own DNA.

Needle
A tiny needle injects the udder cell nucleus into the egg cell.

How would this work?

To re-create a woolly mammoth, genes from preserved remains of mammoths would be put into the DNA of the Asian elephant—the mammoth's closest living relative. The mammoth genes would give the baby traits such as shaggy hair. This would make an "**elemoth**"—an elephant-mammoth hybrid.

Gene splicing
The mammoth genes would be inserted, or **spliced**, into the chromosomes of an Asian elephant.

Asian elephant
The new DNA would be put into an elephant egg and the elemoth baby would grow in a surrogate Asian elephant mother.

Elephant DNA

Return of the
mammoths?

Since 2015, scientists at Harvard University have been looking into bringing the **woolly mammoth** back from **extinction**. They hope to achieve this by using new technology to **replace** elephant genes with woolly mammoth genes.

In 2012, an important **woolly mammoth specimen** was discovered in Russia—by an **11-year-old child**!

Mammoth remains
Scientists are currently extracting DNA from woolly mammoth remains. They would then need to identify different genes and match them up with the elephant genes.

Mammoth gene

LOST FOREVER?

These are some other animal species that have become extinct, but that scientists could potentially bring back to life. Do you think this would be a good idea?

Dinosaurs
Dinosaurs are the ancestors of birds, so we could look at bird DNA to try and figure out how to re-create a dinosaur.

Dodo
The dodo became extinct hundreds of years ago. Some of its DNA has been discovered in remains.

Human diversity

The chance of finding two people—who are not identical twins—with an identical DNA sequence is about the same as tossing a coin and getting heads six million times in a row. Try it!

The human family
Despite the variety, a huge amount of the human genome is the same across the world—**99.9 percent** of it!

May contain Neanderthal!
Most of us contain around 2 percent Neanderthal DNA from our extinct, ancient cousins.

Variety is the spice of life!

Individuals of every species of animal, plant, or microbe all have slightly different **DNA sequences**. This variation is called the **gene pool**. Larger gene pools make species better at **surviving change**.

There are about 3,000,000 differences in the DNA sequences of any two people.

Our genetic history
DNA analysis can be used to trace human origins back to Africa.

Diversity is great!
If we were all the same, our species would be much less healthy!

GENE POOLS

Cheetahs are vulnerable to disease because they have a very small gene pool. About 12,000 years ago, they nearly died out. Only a few individuals survived, and a lot of genetic diversity was lost. Conservation programs run by zoos and other wildlife organizations try to preserve and expand the gene pools of threatened species.

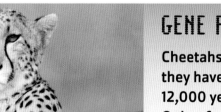

Our genes in
the future

Technology is moving ahead so fast that one day we might even be able to go and live on **another planet!** Our genes, however, will have to keep up with us. What might be useful in the future?

I am always evolving!

Greenland Inuits
Inuit people who live in Greenland have a diet very high in certain kinds of fat. However, they stay fit and healthy because of particular mutations in their genes.

Humans with genetic superpowers

In the world around us today, there are some populations of people that have special powers given to them by their genes. Some of these can be very useful in harsh environments.

Divers
The Bajau people of Southeast Asia can hold their breath for more than 10 minutes to dive for fish! This is because they have mutations that make their spleen, which stores oxygen, larger.

High-altitude adaptation
Himalayan people have evolved to cope with the low levels of oxygen in the air high in the mountains.

Can't feel pain

Some people have inherited pain insensitivity, caused by rare mutations in a few genes. This means that they can't feel the pain of cuts, burns, or even broken bones!

What would you choose?

Which of these superpowers would you like? Deep diving and mountain climbing sound like lots of fun, but wouldn't it be a little dangerous not to feel any pain?

WHAT GENES MIGHT WE STEAL FROM OTHER ORGANISMS?

If we look around at animals and plants in the natural world, we can find some pretty amazing adaptations. Maybe one day we could put genes responsible for some of these adaptations in ourselves and get new superpowers!

Making your own food

Green plants don't need to eat! They use sunlight, water, and carbon dioxide to make food.

Living in the freezing cold

Icefish can survive in chilly Antarctic waters because they produce antifreeze, which stops them from freezing.

63

Timeline of **DNA**

All the things we now know about DNA are thanks to the **hard work** and **creativity** of **scientists**. However, there is still a lot to learn. Maybe you could be on this timeline one day!

ON THE ORIGIN OF SPECIES

Mendel's peas
Mendel did all his experiments on pea plants. He worked on inherited characteristics, such as color and seed shape.

1909: The word **gene** is coined by **Wilhelm Johannsen**.

WHITE BLOOD CELLS

1859

On the Origin of Species

Charles Darwin's book describes his theory of evolution by natural selection—the most important idea ever in biology. However, he knows nothing about DNA's central role in evolution, because it hasn't yet been discovered!

1866

Mechanism of inheritance

Gregor Mendel discovers that **inheritance** involves separate particles—now known as **genes**. His work shows that characteristics are not blended together, like mixing paint colors, but can be separated out again through the generations.

1869

Newfound "nuclein"

Friedrich Miescher identifies what he calls "**nuclein**"—now known as **DNA**—in the nuclei of human white blood cells. He uses pus-soaked bandages from a local hospital as his source of white blood cells.

Morgan's fruit flies

Morgan experimented on fruit flies. He studied how different combinations of characteristics, such as eye color and wing shape, are passed down through the generations.

OSWALD AVERY

1952: Rosalind Franklin photographs crystallized DNA.

Watson and Crick proposed that DNA copies itself by matching bases to each strand of the helix.

DOUBLE HELIX

1911

1944

1953

Chromosome theory

Thomas Hunt Morgan discovers that genes can be physically connected to one another in "linkage groups." He determines that these groups are equivalent to **chromosomes**, and therefore that genes are on chromosomes.

DNA is the hereditary material

No one had yet proved that DNA was the hereditary molecule. **Oswald Avery** and colleagues remove everything from bacterial cells one at a time and find that **only DNA is important for heredity**.

The double helix

James Watson and **Francis Crick** figure out that DNA forms a **double-helix** structure, by studying **Rosalind Franklin**'s X-ray crystallography photographs. Crick bursts into The Eagle pub in Cambridge exclaiming, "We have discovered the secret of life!"

Each codon, or group of three bases, codes for an amino acid.

Nirenberg's genetic codon table

Nirenberg tested all possible codons, or three-letter combinations of the bases A, T, C, and G, to figure out which animo acids they code for.

1961

Three is the magic number

Francis Crick, **Sydney Brenner**, and colleagues prove that a codon—a sequence of bases that codes for one amino acid—is three letters long. This means that DNA forms a **triplet code** to build amino acid chains, which fold themselves up to make proteins.

1965

Cracking the code

Marshall Nirenberg and colleagues figure out **which codons code for each amino acid**. There are 64 possible combinations of three bases, but only 20 amino acids. Some amino acids are coded for by several different codons.

1977

Sequencing at speed

Fred Sanger has the brilliant idea of using the process of DNA copying to **sequence DNA** (work out the order of bases) with great accuracy. His work revolutionizes genetics by letting whole genomes be sequenced and compared.

YEAST CELLS

Fission yeast cells normally divide by splitting in two. However, certain mutants have a faulty cell-division gene and can't divide.

HAEMOPHILUS INFLUENZAE

The bacterium *H. influenzae* has about 1,830,000 bases in its genome. That's roughly a thousandth of the size of the human genome.

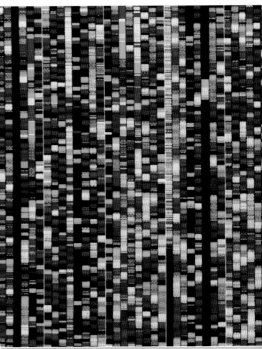

The complete human genome sequence
We now know the complete set of instructions to make a human being. Just think how important this information is!

1987

You're a bit like yeast!

Paul Nurse discovers that you can help mutant yeast cells that can't divide by giving them the human version of the faulty cell-division gene. This means **yeast and human genes are very similar**.

1995

Complete genomes

The era of **genome sequencing** starts with the bacterium *Haemophilus influenzae* in 1995. Yeast follows in 1996. The first animals to be sequenced are *C. elegans* in 1998 and the fruit fly in 2000.

2003

The complete human genome

The first sequence of the human genome involves hundreds of scientists, takes about 13 years, and costs around $2.7 billion! (These days, it takes a few hours and costs a couple of hundred dollars.)

Glossary

These words are helpful to know when talking and learning about DNA.

adaptation
feature of a living thing that helps it survive or reproduce better

allele
particular version of a gene

amino acid
building block of proteins

antennapedia
gene in fruit flies that controls where the legs are formed

bacteria
microscopic, single-celled living things, some of which cause disease (singular: **bacterium**)

base
one of the units that make up DNA. Certain bases attach to each other in DNA's double helix to form **base pairs**

cartilage
tough, flexible tissue in the body

cell
one of the microscopic units that make up living things

cell division
process by which cells are made— a "parent" cell divides to form two new "daughter" cells

characteristic
feature of a living thing controlled by a gene or group of genes

chromosome
threadlike structure in a cell's nucleus that contains DNA. Bacterial chromosomes are loops of DNA and are not in a nucleus

clone
genetically identical copy of a living thing; make a clone of something

codon
sequence of three bases in DNA or RNA that usually codes for an amino acid

conservation
protection of animals, plants, and their habitats in the natural world

contaminate
make something dirty or infected by touching it or mixing with it

cystic fibrosis
genetic disorder affecting the lungs

DNA (deoxyribonucleic acid)
molecule in cells that holds the instructions for life. It is made up of sequences of the bases adenine, thymine, cytosine, and guanine, and a sugar-phosphate backbone

DNA polymerase
protein that helps DNA copy itself

DNA profile
characteristics of someone's DNA sequence based on the order of its bases. Also called a DNA "fingerprint"

dominant
used to describe an allele of a gene that has priority over another allele

double helix
shape of the DNA molecule, like a ladder twisted to the right

egg
female sex cell

evolution
process of change in generations of living things over time that occurs due to **natural selection** and leads to the creation of new species

extinction
permanent disappearance of a population or species

fertilize
fuse male and female sex cells to form a new living thing

gene
section of DNA that carries the code to make a protein

gene editing
inserting, removing, or altering DNA in a living thing

gene pool
total of all the genetic variation of a population or species

gene therapy
insertion of normal genes to replace faulty or missing genes in our cells

genome
complete set of the DNA in a living thing

hybrid
offspring produced by the breeding of two different species

immune system
system through which an organism gets rid of invaders, such as germs

inheritance
characteristics received from parents through the passing on of their genes. The process of inheritance is called **heredity**

insulin
protein that balances the level of sugar in a living thing's blood

linkage group
genes on the same chromosome, usually inherited as a group

membrane
thin layer that acts as a boundary

microscope
instrument used for looking at very tiny, or **microscopic**, objects

mitochondria
tiny units inside cells that supply the energy to drive the cell's processes (singular: **mitochondrion**)

model organism
species widely used in laboratories to study biology

molecule
group of elements, such as carbon and hydrogen, bonded together

mutation
change to a gene that results in genetic variation if it is inherited. Living things with a mutation are called **mutants**

natural selection
idea that living things with the most favorable characteristics are more likely to survive and reproduce

nematode
any of a group of worms that includes the model organism *C. elegans*

Nobel Prize
award for groundbreaking work in several fields, including physiology or medicine, chemistry, and peace

nucleus
central part of a cell that contains the chromosomes (plural: **nuclei**)

organism
living thing. Types of organism include animals, plants, fungi, protists, and bacteria. Viruses are not usually thought of as "living"

protein
large molecule made up of one or more chains of amino acids

ribosome
particle made of RNA and protein in cells that, with the help of RNA, assembles proteins

RNA (ribonucleic acid)
molecule similar to DNA but with a different sugar in its backbone and the base uracil instead of thymine. Messenger RNA (mRNA) is a copy of DNA code, and transfer RNA (tRNA) brings amino acids to ribosomes

selective breeding
controlled breeding of animals and plants to produce characteristics useful or desirable to humans

sequence
specific order of bases in a strand of DNA; to determine the order of the bases in a strand of DNA

species
group of related living things able to breed together

sperm
male sex cell

spleen
body organ that removes old red blood cells and stores blood. It also has a role in the immune system

splice
insert a gene from one living thing into the DNA of another

transcription
process in which the genetic code stored in DNA is copied into a molecule of messenger RNA

translation
process in which ribosomes assemble chains of amino acids by reading the genetic code of mRNA

transparent
another word for see-through

triplet code
genetic code in which codons (three bases in a precise order in DNA or RNA) code for specific amino acids

udder
milk-producing organ with teats on the underside of sheep and cows

ultraviolet (UV)
form of radiation invisible to humans that's given off by the sun

virus
smallest type of microbe, consisting of DNA or RNA wrapped in protein. Viruses reproduce in living things

X-ray crystallography
scientific way of figuring out the structure of a molecule (in a crystal form) by using X-rays

Index

Acknowledgments

DK would like to thank Polly Goodman for proofreading and Helen Peters for compiling the index.

The authors would like to acknowledge Cristina Fonseca at the Genetics Society and the Royal Institution of Great Britain for inspiration and ideas for **Our genes in the future** on pages 62–63.

Professor Alison Woollard would like to dedicate this book to her two daughters, Alice and Emily, in the hope that she's passed on good genes!

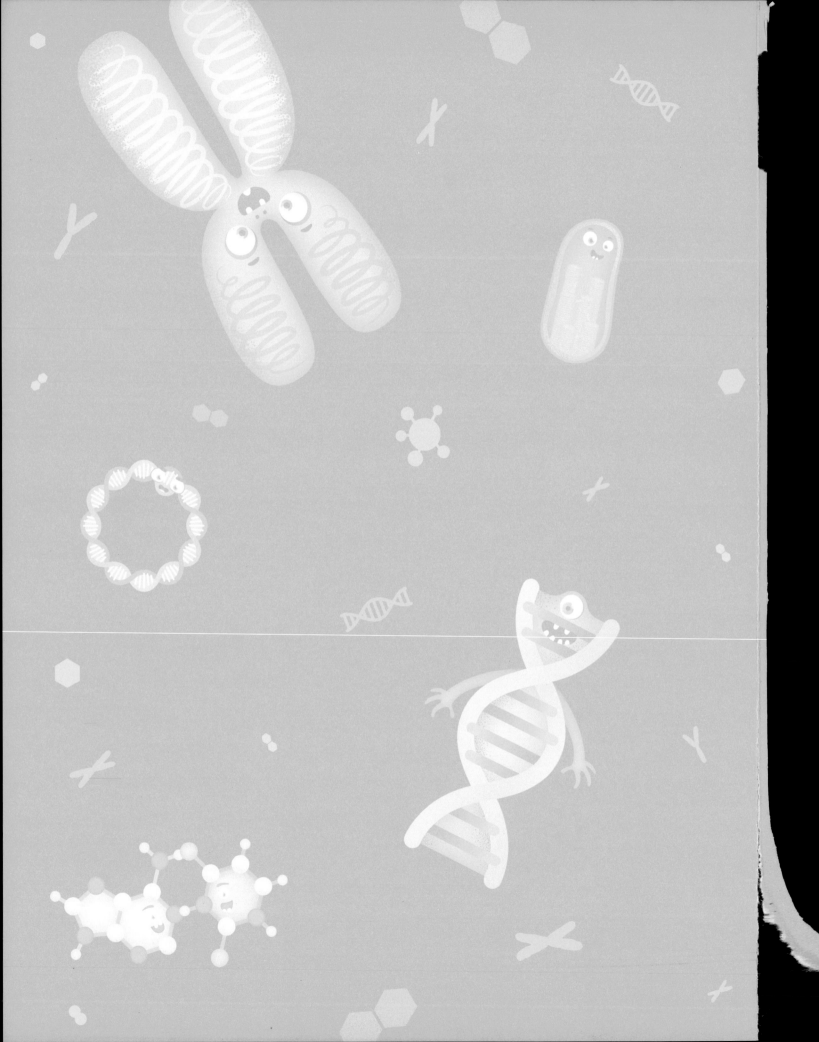